THE MIAMISBURG & GERMANTOWN TRACTION COMPANY
(THE TWIN VALLEY LINE)

By HERB PENCE, JR.

No electric line is as intriguing to Southwestern Ohio rail historians as the route between Miamisburg and Germantown. It was owned by its parent company for only nine months, was consolidated into a larger operation, was severed from its rail connections by a flood, and finally sold for scrap at the courthouse door. All this happened in 18 years.

Prior to 1901, the residents of Germantown, in southwestern Montgomery County, had two alternatives when undertaking a trip to Dayton. They could ride the Cincinnati Northern (NYC System) and change trains for the rest of the journey at Franklin or West Alexandria, or they could ride a "bus" owned by Henry Kamp's Livery Stable over the present State Route 725 between Germantown and Miamisburg to catch the Southern Ohio Traction. Neither way was very enticing from a comfort or convenience standpoint.

Miamisburg businessmen decided that an electric line between their town and Germantown would be a good investment. There was an opportunity for a direct profit from an interurban and their businesses would also be helped by the increased traffic.

On September 20, 1900, the Miamisburg City Council passed an ordinance permitting the Miamisburg & Germantown Traction Company to operate on Linden Avenue, from the bridge to Main Street, a distance of one block. During the same period, the County granted the M&G a 25-year franchise. It required that the County Surveyor establish the track centerline and do grading engineering work. On gravelled roads which were later paved, the M&G was required to pave, with like material, the span between the rails and twenty inches on either side. A franchise tax of $25.00 per mile of road under county supervision over which the M&G operated

The Miamisburg end of the traction line was only one block long--on Linden Avenue from Main Street to the Miami River bridge --but within that distance it included a steep grade onto the bridge and interchange sidings on the south (to the left in the picture) with the Southern Ohio Traction Co. Tracks were never laid on this bridge which was new after the traction bridge was lost in the 1913 flood. (R. M. Wagner)

Riverview Drive and Short Hill Road across the river from Miamisburg appeared more rustic early in the century when car 14 waited there (left, Herb Pence, Jr. Collection) than it does today (Below, R. M. Wagner) but Short Hill Road is just as steep. The Traction crossed the bridge and turned south, or left, onto Riverview and passed the CH&D (B&O) R. R. station, the brick building, for a short distance and then headed west on private right-of-way.

was to be collected. The speed was set at a maximum of 25 mph. with quarter mile stopping points. Finally, the cars were limited to an eight-foot width and 20-ton weight.

Construction began immediately. The general contractor was apparently John Kershner, Dayton, Ohio. He received help from a number of individuals and organizations. The Southern Ohio Traction Company, the connecting line in Miamisburg, was intensely interested in the M&G. Its employees helped with the construction. The M&G assumed part of the cost of the new Linden Avenue bridge, built to replace a wooden one. Sam Mays was in charge of construction. Principal assistants in engineering were Robert Kline, George Riley, and Sam Moore. Mr. Moore later became City Engineer of Miamisburg.

On June 13, 1901, it was announced that the construction was complete. Line length was five miles; the rail was 60 lb. made by Carnegie Steel. The overhead was supported by wooden poles, purchased from H. Wantz, Miamisburg, and Valentine Clark, Chicago, Illinois. Capitalization was $50,000 gold bonds in $1,000 denomination, issued 1901, interest

TWO OHIO TRACTIONS

EDITED BY RICHARD AND BIRDELLA WAGNER

INTRODUCTION

It was an established fact in America that growth and prosperity had followed the construction of railroads. The building boom at the century's beginning was in ELECTRIC railroads and it was reported that high profits were to be earned. In 1900 the population of Miamisburg had not yet reached 4,000 and Germantown's was listed at only 1702, but opportunity seemed to be knocking!

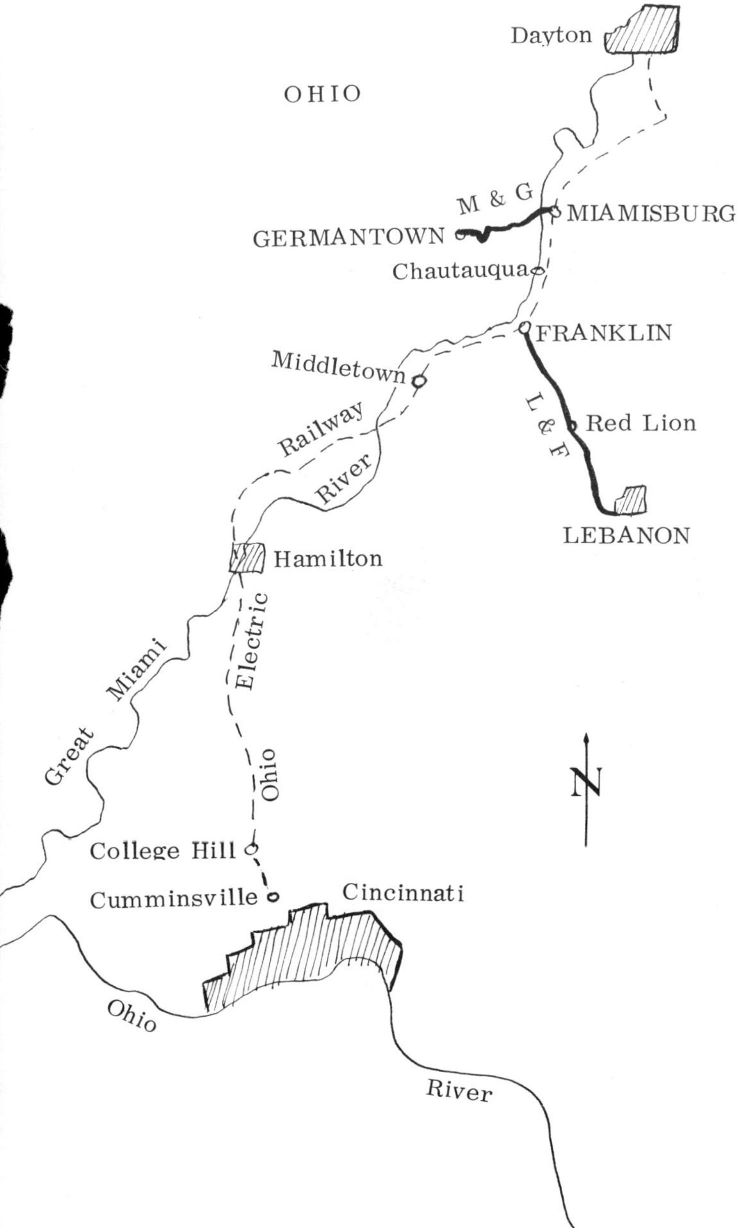

In 1901, George S. Davis writing for the STREET RAILWAY JOURNAL figured that franchises and rights-of-way had been secured for 4,800 miles of electric railways in Ohio. In some portions of the State, he said, there were more electric railway projects than could be kept track of by a United States census official. He quoted from a country newspaper in the northern part of the State, "Electric railway men are thicker than flies in summer these days, and they appear to have entirely superseded the lightning rod agents of former days. The progressive farmers in these parts all have special rooms set for conferences with railway promoters, and hardly a day passes but they are called into use. A well dressed stranger drives up, and the farmer at once ushers him into the conference room, where paper and pen are kept. The right of way through farm or along highway is signed, and the promoter passes on to the next with neatness and despatch."

One franchise which was secured was by the Dayton, Germantown & Hamilton Railway for private right-of-way between Dayton and Middletown for a road promised to be built "at once" but which never materialized. It was promoted by J. O. Arnold and T. C. Lindsay of Dayton, said to be backed by the Cincinnati Hamilton & Dayton steam railroad which had lost much suburban business to the Southern Ohio Traction Company.

A network of loosely connected, overlapping and sometimes clashing, syndicates were promoting the electric railways, roughly the Everett-Moore group in the northern part of Ohio, the Appleyard interests centrally, and Pomeroy-Mandelbaum in the southern section. The chief aim of the latter was to build a road from Cincinnati to Toledo and to Cleveland. Its Southern Ohio Traction was considered one of the best in the State. In competition Mr. Appleyard controlled the steam road from Dayton to Lebanon which he planned to electrify and extend.

Our TWO OHIO TRACTIONS, the Miamisburg & Germantown and the Lebanon & Franklin, both made connections with the Southern Ohio (which later became part of the huge Ohio Electric and eventually part of the Cincinnati & Lake Erie, one of the most colorful railways in the country.) Although not all roads that were projected in Ohio were built, the two little lines reported here served the people along their routes in a unique and satisfying way even though they lasted less than two decades.

1

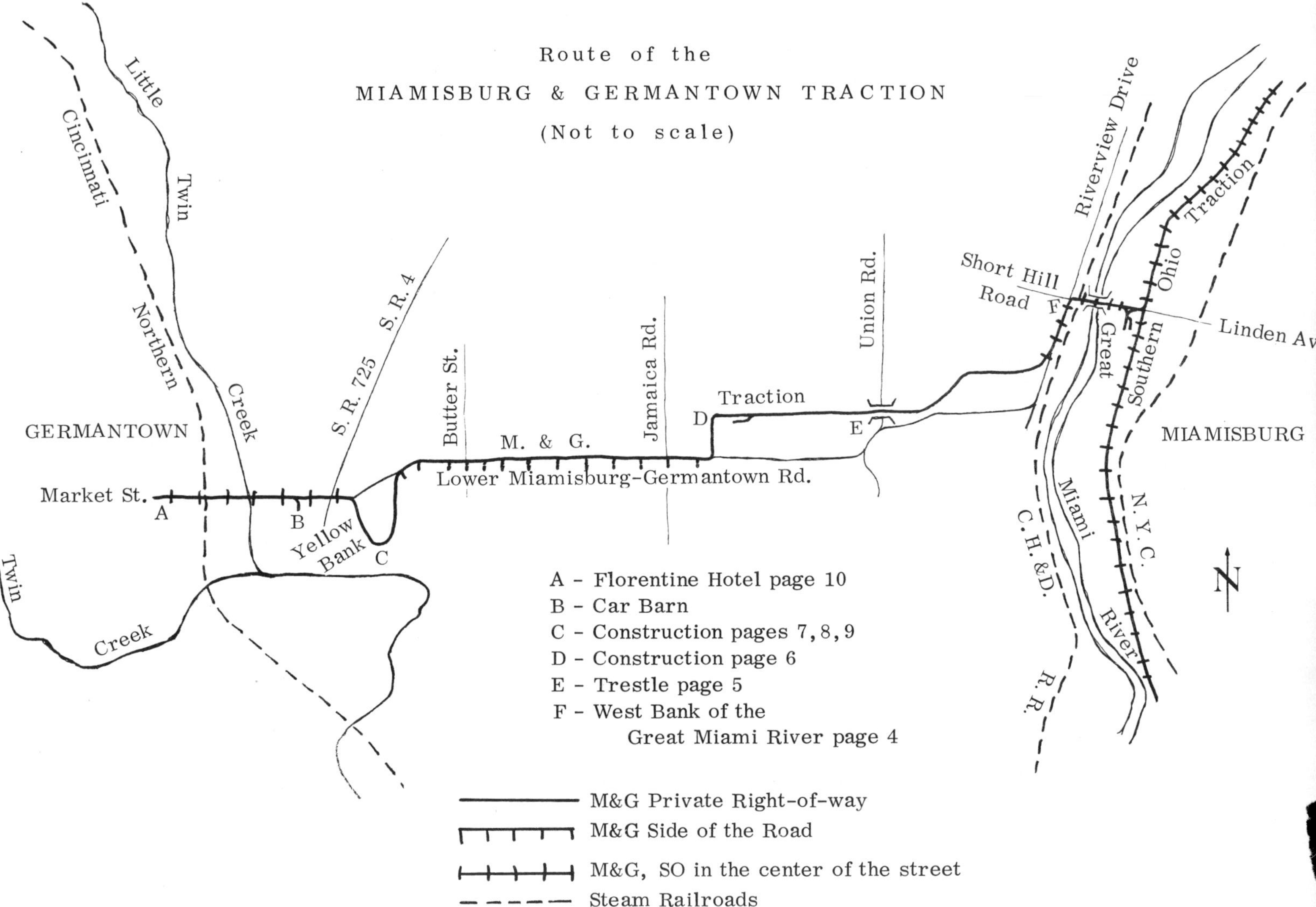

Herb Pence, Jr., is a long time resident of Cincinnati who is presently Director of Marketing, Tidewater Metro Transit, Norfolk, Virginia. He is a freelance writer in his free time, concentrating on transportation subjects. Mr. Pence has an exceptional interest in traction subjects in the Southwestern Ohio area. His historical pieces have appeared in The Cincinnati Enquirer and The Bulletin, published by the Railway and Locomotive Historical Society.

FOREWORD

As a Southwestern Ohio traction fan, I had heard many stories regarding the "Germantown Line". No one seemed to have the accurate story. My wife, Judy, is a native of Miamisburg and on the frequent trips to visit her parents, I took the opportunity to research this history.

Many people helped me. Their names appear on photo credits or in the text of the history. Without their patience and interest, the story of "The Twin Valley Line" would not yet be written.

Herb Pence, Jr.
January 31, 1974

The line's private right-of-way took it up the hill and across Union Road. The trestle over Union Rd. had sturdy abutments. In the scene above the photographer's back is to the Lower Germantown Road, which is beyond the houses at the foot of Union Road hill in the picture at left. This shows the stone pier 55 years after the traction line had been abandoned. (Top, source unknown, Herb Pence, Jr. Col.; left, R. M. Wagner)

Across the countryside on private right-of-way, construction of the railway took a minimum of farm land. At left, work progresses on top of the hill midway between the two valleys, looking toward Miamisburg.

The overhead was hung first and the work car "Grasshopper" brought materials to the construction crew as far as the track was laid. (All three, from glass plate negatives owned by Robert Ingabrand, Germantown)

The tracks came north from Lower Germantown Road across the fields a little east of Jamaica Road and then curved eastward toward the trestle over Union Road, thence down the hill toward Miamisburg.

5% payable in June and December, due December 1, 1911, and later extended to July 1, 1922. The Cincinnati Trust Company was Trustee. The rolling stock was comprised of two combine cars, one express motor, and one work car.

Terminal stations were the Florentine Hotel in Germantown and Gwinner's Drug Store in Miamisburg. Arnold Gwinner was also the line's General Manager. The M&G had a single track barn located at 935 East Market Street, the extreme eastern end of Germantown. It was not built until 1902. It is not known how the cars were serviced or where they were stored before then.

The route left Miamisburg, crossing the Linden Avenue bridge. It turned left on Riverview Drive for a short distance, then turned right to private right-of-way up a hill in a westerly and southwesterly direction to Union Road. The line crossed Union Road on a substantial trestle. It followed the back property line of the Charles Hoerner (or Cross) farm, where a single stub-end passing siding was located. Then the line turned south for a quarter of a mile to the Lower Miamisburg-Germantown Road on which it turned west. At Jamaica Road the right-of-way was so close to the fence that if the farmer didn't have the gate closed a passing car would tear it off. The line continued along the south side of the Lower Miamisburg-Germantown Road to a point near the top of the hill at "Yellow Bank". (The M&G took

its nickname "Twin Valley Line" from Twin Creek which created "Yellow Bank" by erosion over many centuries.) The private right-of-way can still be traced by following the power line which heads south. The line descended "Yellow Bank" in a deep cut. Then the tracks entered the center of the Lower Miamisburg-Germantown Road, now called East Market Street, for the entrance into Germantown.

As seen in the construction photos, the overhead was installed first. The power was to be purchased from the Southern Ohio, probably originating in the power house at Franklin.

On June 22, 1901, the first scheduled car operated to Germantown. Twenty-eight minutes was required for a trip. The schedule called for trips leaving Miamisburg every hour on the half-hour from 6:30 a.m. to 11:30 p.m. Germantown service was from 6:00 a.m. until 11:00 p.m. It was not until the fall of 1901 that the crossing was installed at the Cincinnati Northern (NYC), which permitted service the final three blocks to the Florentine Hotel. The fare was 10¢ for the entire line, 5¢ if the passenger did not cross Jamaica Road. Commutation tickets were sold.

The operator was supposed to give a blast on the whistle when a car approached Jamaica Road and Lower Germantown Road where a farm house was situated near the corner. When the farmer's sister took sick, the car would stop and the conductor would

The depth of the cut into Yellow Bank hill can be judged by the men standing in it. Ballast, ties and rail were yet to be laid but the tall trolley poles with overhead wire in place mark a slight curve the other direction (in lower photo) for the descent to the road into Germantown. (Glass plate negatives owned by Robert Ingabrand, Germantown)

Next page
→

Today the hill is there but the right-of-way along its side (top) is so overgrown as to be almost obliterated. The spot where the tracks re-entered the Lower Miamisburg-Germantown Road is marked (center) by a speed limit sign. The road proceeds into Germantown (bottom) where it becomes Market Street and crosses Twin Creek before arriving in the center of town.
(R. M. Wagner)

SPEED
LIMIT
25

STOP

The Florentine Hotel, the Old Leighty House, on the south side of Market Street in Germantown was the M&G station. Here Mike Ryan (white shirt) is in front of the hotel; Josephine Orth is in the buggy with Ed Lang standing behind it; the motorman in the light jacket is Claude Wagner. Car 102 advertises the Montgomery County Fair in Dayton on September 8, 9, 10, 11 on its fender and life guard. The date of the photo is probably September, 1904. Note the auto with the single headlight. (R. E. Oblinger, First National Bank of Germantown, and Richard A. Lenehan)

Some of the M&G equipment had a longer life than the traction line itself. A twin of the car in front of the
Florentine Hotel (left), M&G car 101 is shown above about 1936 as car No. 794 of the Dayton & Western
Traction Company at their shops at West Alexandria. The Barney & Smith trucks had been exchanged for
MCB type trucks but otherwise the former M&G combine retained the characteristics as when it served
the residents and businesses of Miamisburg and Germantown. (Richard A. Lenehan Collection)

alight to wave the car across when all was clear so
as not to disturb the sick woman. (That was courtesy
extended in a bygone era!)

The M&G was quite successful. According to
Poor's Manual, 1902, the Southern Ohio purchased
the line for $75,000 in February, 1902. Remember,
it was capitalized at $50,000. Financial results for
the first nine months show the M&G earned $4,337
on income of $8,845. Not a bad return!

Service under the SO was improved. Through
service to Dayton was tried in 1904-5 for six months.
The cars from Germantown operated as the first
section ahead of main line cars coming from Franklin. They picked up until full, then operated express
into Dayton.

The corporate history has many twists and turns.
The M&G was incorporated in 1900. It was sold to
and became a subsidiary of the Southern Ohio Trac-
tion Company in 1902. This later became the Cin-
cinnati, Dayton & Toledo Traction Company. On
January 24, 1905, the Cincinnati Northern Traction
Company was incorporated. The CN leased all the
property of the Hamilton and Lindenwald Electric
Transit Company; Cincinnati Northwestern Railway;
Dayton Traction; Cincinnati, Dayton and Toledo
Traction; and the Cincinnati and Hamilton Electric
Railway Company.

Apparently extra movements were phone dis-
patched; there is no record of telegraphers. Freight
service was handled by the express car. Claude
Wagner was the express conductor and his motorman
was Butch Weidner. A major shipper was the Mud
Lick Distillery. This interesting building is still
standing and is used as a private museum. The
M&G carried shipments for the U.S. Express Co.
and the Southern Ohio Express Co. A brief notice
in the Miamisburg News dated August 1, 1907,
stated that effective September 1, 1907, U.S. Mail
would no longer be carried on the M&G.

At the beginning of 1909, the schedule was slightly changed. The first car left Germantown at 5:55 a.m. with hourly service until 8:55 p.m. then 10:55 p.m. and 12:25 a.m. Corresponding service from Miamisburg began at 6:05 a.m., ran hourly until 9:05 p.m., then 11:42, and one car after midnight.

In the spring of 1913, the Great Miami River went on a rampage. One result was the destruction of the Linden Avenue bridge in Miamisburg. Fortunately, one car, No. 14, was left on the line. The CH&D (B&O) railroad station had been washed away. For a substitute station a boxcar was placed at the intersection of Riverview Drive and Short Hill Road and this was also used as the interurban station.

Carl Krug remembers servicing car No. 14. He was an armature winder in the shops at First and * Tremont, Dayton. When the motors had to be changed he went out and did it "in a ditch". There is some question whether or not the adjacent CH&D railroad was ever contacted concerning the transportation of car No. 14 to Dayton for shop service. In any event, the car was not to leave the line for six years. Harry Shank, a one-time union president, said that the car would be out of service for days at a time. When the line was abandoned, No. 14 was apparently scrapped.

Harry Shank also remembers working the M&G following his hiring out on the Ohio Electric Railway June 29, 1916. At that time the OE owned the M&G. In final service schedules began at 6:00 a.m. from Germantown with three trips. Then there was a lapse until afternoon, with hourly trips until 9:00 p.m. There was no Sunday service. The fares rose from 10¢ straight, with reduced commutation tickets, to 20¢ straight, "no tickets, no receipts, only cash".

In the early days of the line, the work car "Grasshopper" was used for excursion service. It was decorated and carried passengers as far as the bridge to Chautauqua, north of Franklin. It was also used to carry rooters from Germantown to a "ball field" at the top of "Yellow Bank". During World War I the land was used as a "flying field". Dayton, thanks to the Wright Brothers, was the cradle of aviation; it was natural that training fields were built nearby.

The war traffic proved to be only a temporary boon to the railway; afterwards the line suffered from neglect. When interest was not paid on bonds, a public sale was ordered. W. E. Hutton, President of the Cincinnati & Dayton Traction Company which succeeded the Ohio Electric in 1918, was ordered to sell the line. Under Ohio law, the bondholders had to offer 2/3 of the value. The appraised value was $18,000. The public sale was held at the Montgomery County Courthouse door in September, 1919; on December 12, 1919, the M&G was abandoned. Area residents later purchased ties and poles.

The final chapter of the M&G, the Twin Valley Line, closes in the Western Ohio Sand and Gravel Company, located south of Germantown. According to Robert Groves, he helped dig the abandoned rails from the pavement in Germantown east to the bottom of the hill at "Yellow Bank". Later at the gravel plant, he helped lay down the rail. In the 1920's Mr. Groves operated a small steam locomotive over the same rails he had ridden as a small boy in an interurban.

          * Barney & Smith

Car No. 14 was left high and dry on the west side of the river after the bridge was destroyed in the 1913 flood. It waits on Riverview Drive near Short Hill Road with the crew, Irvin Roof, motorman, and Lawrence Hardin, conductor.
(Charles V. Hess Collection)

Irvin Roof worked for the Cincinnati & Lake Erie and saw it to the finish. Here he exchanges his car, No. 100, for Mr. Bell's (man on left) No. 103, at 12:15 a.m. on Sunday, May 14th, 1939, for his next to last trip - to Moraine, where he changed cars with Roy Collins. Mr. Roof then took car No. 101 to Miamisburg - his final run.
(Clayton Lyday, David L. McNeil Collection)

Employees and other people closely associated with the Miamisburg & Germantown Traction Company compiled by Herb Pence, Jr.:

Warren Bicknell, General Manager of Southern Ohio Traction Co.
Bert Coleman, Motorman, also with Cincinnati & Lake Erie
C. W. Dodds, President
James Egan, Conductor, also with Cincinnati & Lake Erie
George Gemmaka, Engineer
Arnold Gwinner, General Manager
Mr. Greathouse, Motorman
Al Gullum, Motorman, also with Cincinnati & Lake Erie
William Hamilton, Conductor, also with Cincinnati & Lake Erie
Lawrence Hardin, Conductor, also with Cincinnati & Lake Erie
William (Joe) Hauser, Motorman
Mr. Herman, Motorman
John Kershner, General Contractor, Dayton
Robert Kline, Engineer
Carl Krug, Shopman
J. H. Mays, Vice President
Sam Mays, in charge of construction
W. A. Mays, Secretary
Sam Moore, designed special track work
Billy Myers, Motorman
"Dad" Newton, Conductor
Mr. Overcash
Jerry Phillips, Superintendent of Overhead, Southern Ohio Traction
Charles "Shorty" Raymond, Motorman, also with Cincinnati & Lake Erie
George Riley, tangent track work
Irvin Roof, Motorman, also with Cincinnati & Lake Erie
Mrs. Gert Rosebaum, Ticket Clerk, Miamisburg
Clarence Rosebaum, Conductor
Mr. Schlenker, Ticket Agent, Germantown
Harry Shank, Conductor
Mr. Sheits, Lineman
Mr. Snider
Wilmore Spires, Superintendent of Grading, Southern Ohio Traction
Jeff Stokes, in charge of bridges and culverts
Perry Swartzel, Conductor
Claude Wagner, Conductor and Motorman
Theodore Weaver, Conductor
William (Butch) Weidner, Motorman
Fred Wright, Conductor
Robert Yarnell
Mr. Youngerman, Conductor

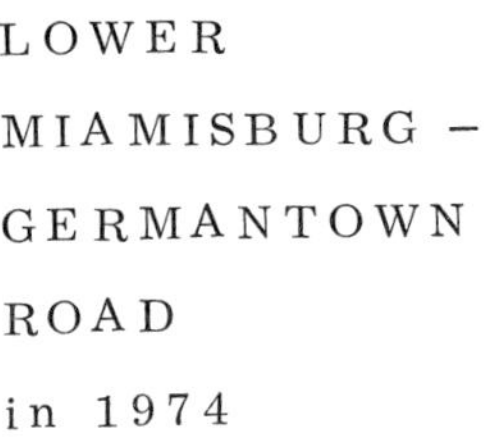

Traces of the traction
line can still be
detected along the
side of the road in
these pictures.
(All, R. M. Wagner)

While driving through
the beautiful Ohio
countryside the hills
seem gentle and the
curves slight but the
building and operating
of an electric railway
over this terrain in
1900 was a triumph
for engineering and
electricity.

Even when it is dim, a picture from the past can stir memories. This scene is car 14 in Germantown early in the century. It brought out the recollection that, "It frequently became necessary for the more muscular passengers to get out and push the car over the hump or walk the rest of the way into town. This always seemed to happen on the trip into Germantown."
(Richard A. Lenehan Collection)

CHRONOLOGY OF THE MIAMISBURG & GERMANTOWN TRACTION COMPANY OWNERSHIP
Compiled by R. M. Wagner and R. A. Lenehan

1900-1901 The Miamisburg & Germantown Traction Company was organized by local interests. Investors included Robert Kline, Tom Seltz, Ed Gephart, Fred Rike, Chester Bolser, and Mrs. Kumler. These men signed the articles of incorporation filed the first day of August, 1900: Wm. A. Mays, C. W. Dodds, S. H. Mays, and Albert J. Dwyer.

1902 The Miamisburg & Germantown was sold to the Pomeroy-Mandelbaum syndicate and became part of the Southern Ohio Traction Company (organized 1900) which had absorbed the Dayton Traction Company operating to the south corporation line of Miamisburg from the city of Dayton, having been incorporated in 1893 by Wm. Huffman, Stephen J. Patterson, Fred. Reibold, Oscar M. Gottschall, Dennis Dwyer, Wm. A. Mays, Oren Britt Brown, and Walter W. Smith. It had also absorbed the Cincinnati & Miami Valley Traction Company operating from the city of Hamilton to the south corporation line of Miamisburg having been incorporated in 1896 by Dennis Dwyer, Wm. A. Mays, Albert Emanuel, Jno. T. Wolf and Albert J. Dwyer.

1902-4 The Miamisburg & Germantown, as part of the Southern Ohio, consolidated into the Cincinnati, Dayton & Toledo Traction Company whose officers included Will Christy, M. J. Mandelbaum, Otto Miller, H. C. Lang, F. T. Pomeroy, and subsequently, Geo. B. Cox, W. Kesley Schoepf and J. B. Foraker.

1905-07 The Miamisburg & Germantown, as part of the CD&T, came under control of the Schoepf-McGowan syndicate and became known as the Cincinnati Northern Traction Company which also included the Hamilton & Lindenwald Electric Transit Company, the Cincinnati Northwestern and the Cincinnati & Hamilton.

1907-1917 The Miamisburg & Germantown as part of the Cincinnati Northern was leased to the Ohio Electric Railway Company, a larger Schoepf-McGowan enterprise which grew to over 600 miles of electric railways before going into receivership in 1917.

1918 The Miamisburg & Germantown, along with properties of the old Cincinnati Northern, became the Cincinnati & Dayton Traction Company under Receiver Benton S. Oppenheimer and officers J. M. Hutton, Otto Armleader, Claude Ashbrook, Leo Van Lahr, M. Ackerman, C. A. Hamilton (of Miamisburg), J. M. Brick. The Chief Engineer at Lindenwald was J. P. Davis and the Master Mechanic at O'Neils Car Shops was M. Schoenhals.

1919 The Miamisburg & Germantown segment of the C&D was abandoned but other parts of the C&D later became the famed Cincinnati & Lake Erie.

Cincinnati, Dayton & Toledo Traction Company express freight motor car No. 105 probably hauled shipments from the Mud Lick Distillery of Germantown as well as many other products. The loading cart is lettered "Southern Ohio". A guess would set the date about 1905. (Herb Pence, Jr. Collection)

MIAMISBURG & GERMANTOWN ROSTER OF EQUIPMENT
Compiled by Herb Pence, Jr.

Car Nos.

101–102 Combines built by Barney & Smith, Dayton, Ohio
The best information from Dayton traction fans is that these cars were
sold about 1903 to the Dayton & Western for use on the New Paris branch.
This is understandable, in view of the cars being small and odd on a larger system.
Dr. Reed Prugh, Dayton, suggests the following renumberings and ownership:
On Ohio Electric subsidiary Dayton & Western, they became 55 and 56; approximately
1920 the D&W was returned to the Winters' family (banking) in Dayton and the cars
became 792 and 793; later 792 and D&W center cab 794 swapped numbers. When
the cars became 792-3, they were rebuilt into milk and dispatch cars and also used
as auxiliary freight motors. About 1929, 793 was withdrawn from service and is
believed to have been rebuilt into steel sheathed freight motor 796 on the D&W.
When the Indiana Railroad took over the D&W, 796 was renumbered 737 and
remained on the property until 1940. On the other hand, 794 remained at their
West Alexandria barn until 1936, when it was scrapped.

"GRASSHOPPER" Center cab work car, used during line construction. It possibly was
purchased from the Southern Ohio since that company's employees were used
in the M&G construction. This car might have been SO 100, possibly later Cincinnati
& Dayton 701, and scrapped in 1923. On special occasions it was decorated and
used in excursion service.

Express Car Virtually nothing is known about this car. It could have been similar to Cincinnati,
Dayton & Toledo's No. 105.

14 Although this car is not an original car for the line, it was associated with the M&G
for the longest period of time. It was built by Kuhlman Car Company of Cleveland
for the Cincinnati & Hamilton in 1898. In 1913 it was stranded when the Linden
Avenue bridge was demolished, and finally junked when the line was sold in 1919.

Editor's Note: All cars were double-end, i.e., they could run in either direction by
putting the proper trolley pole on the wire. The line had no loops for turning the
cars around. Track gauge was 4'-8$\frac{1}{2}$"; total track was 5 miles.

The route between Dayton
and Cincinnati included
Miamisburg and Germantown
in 1907 on a Cincinnati
Northern Traction ticket.
(C. L. Bandy Collection)

THE CINCINNATI NORTHERN TRACTION CO.
GOOD FOR ONE RIDE
BETWEEN STATIONS PUNCHED AND GOOD ONLY FOR THE
November 1907
Month of
Not good unless detached by the Conductor.
F. J. Sloat, Gen'l Mgr.
Book No. 1535
Ticket No. 45

DAYTON
EBYS
Springboro Road
GERMANTOWN
Alexandersville
West Carrollton
MIAMISBURG
SHEPHERDS
CHAUTAUQUA
FRANKLIN
RIVERSIDE
STATE DAM
MIDDLETOWN
ENGLESIDE
TRENTON
BUSENBARK
OVERPECK
OHLINGERS
HAMILTON
LINDENWALD
SYMMES CORNER
COUNTY LINE
PLEASANT RUN
Houstons Lane
TAYLOR CREEK
New Burlington
MT. HEALTHY
COLLEGE HILL
CINCINNATI

Car 102, a combination coach and baggage car, was photographed on Market Street in Germantown sometime after the fall of 1901 when the line reached that point.   (The wrong date was written on the face of the picture.)   The roof sign advises destinations of "Dayton, Miamisburg & Germantown".   Perry Swartzel was the conductor and Bert Coleman the motorman. (Western Studio, Germantown)

As Ohio Electric 55, ex-M&G 101, the Barney & Smith car body remained virtually unchanged but the trucks had been "beefed up" and air tanks added for air brakes replacing the original hand brakes.   Also note the hand rail on the end windows and the big wood pilot, typical of OE.   (Reed C. Prugh)

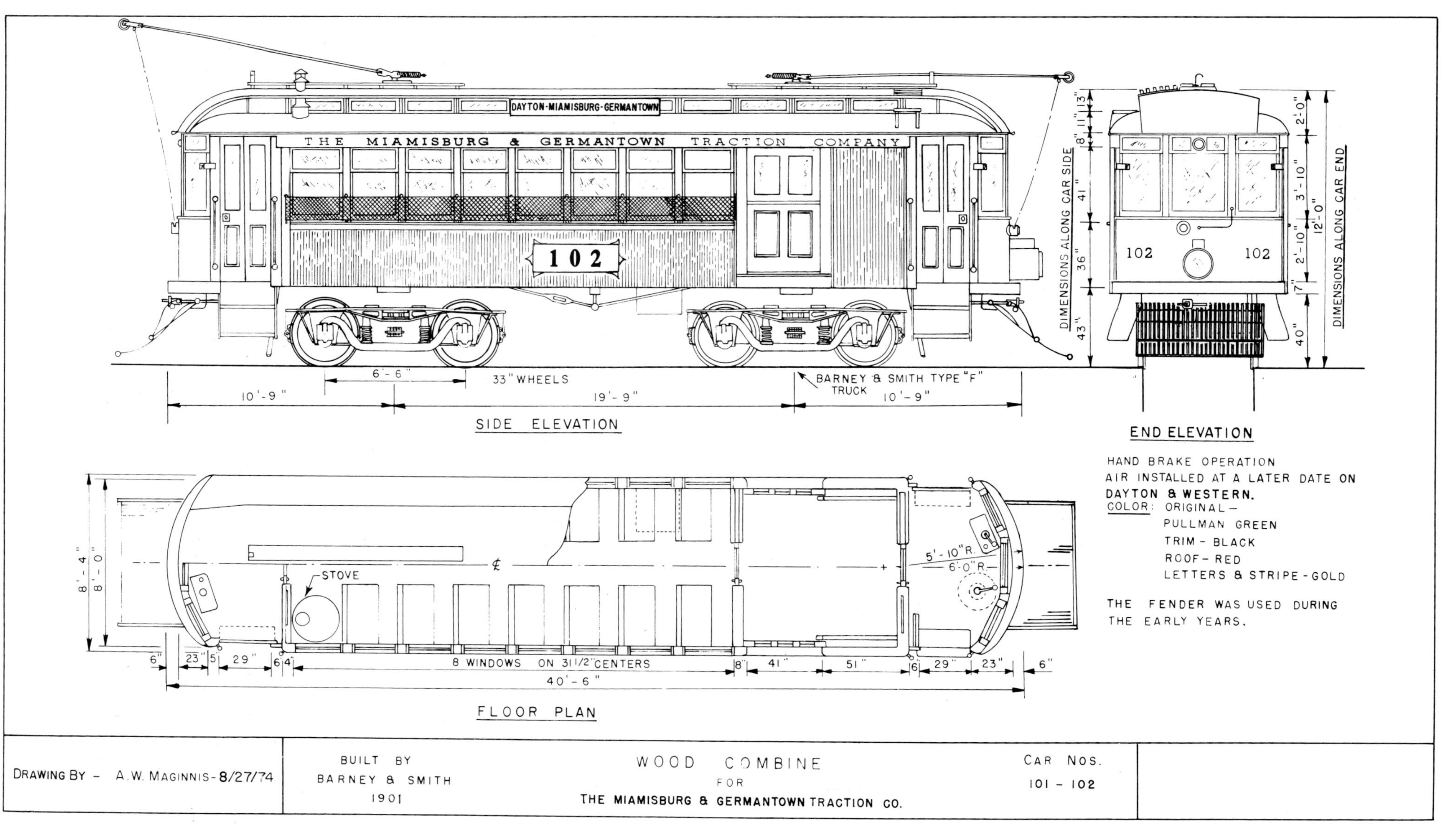

DAYTON-MIAMISBURG-GERMANTOWN
THE MIAMISBURG & GERMANTOWN TRACTION COMPANY
102
6'-6"
33" WHEELS
10'-9"
19'-9"
BARNEY & SMITH TYPE "F"
TRUCK
10'-9"
SIDE ELEVATION
DIMENSIONS ALONG CAR SIDE
43"
36"
41"
8"
11"
13"
102
102
DIMENSIONS ALONG CAR END
2'-0"
3'-10"
12'-0"
2'-10"
7"
40"
END ELEVATION
HAND BRAKE OPERATION
AIR INSTALLED AT A LATER DATE ON
DAYTON & WESTERN.
COLOR: ORIGINAL —
PULLMAN GREEN
TRIM - BLACK
ROOF - RED
LETTERS & STRIPE - GOLD
THE FENDER WAS USED DURING
THE EARLY YEARS.
STOVE
8'-4"
8'-0"
6"
23"
5"
29"
6'4"
8 WINDOWS ON 31½" CENTERS
40'-6"
8"
41"
51"
6"
29"
23"
6"
5'-10"R
6'-0"R
FLOOR PLAN
DRAWING BY - A.W. MAGINNIS - 8/27/74
BUILT BY
BARNEY & SMITH
1901
WOOD COMBINE
FOR
THE MIAMISBURG & GERMANTOWN TRACTION CO.
CAR NOS.
101 - 102

C. D. & T. TRACTION CO.

GOING SOUTH BETWEE[N]

Dayton, Miamisburg, Germantown, Franklin, Lebanon, Mi[ddletown …]

SOUTH BOUND. READ DOWN.

Station	Miles	No. 2	No. 4	No. 6	No. 8	No. 8	No. 10	No. 14	No. 16	No. 20	No. 22	No. 24	No. 26	No. 28	No. 32	No. 34	No. 38	No. 40	No. 42	No. 44	No. 46	No. 50	No. 52	No. 54	No. 56	No. 58	No. 60	No. 62	No. 64	No. 66	No. 68	No. 70	No. 72
Class		D	D Ex.S	D Ex.S	D*	D* Ex.S	D* Ex.S	D Ex.S	D	D Ex.S	D	D Ex.S	D	D	D	D	D	D	D	D	D	D	D	D	D	D	D	D	D	D	D	D	D
		A M	A M	A M	A M	A M	A M	A M	A M	A M	A M	A M	A M	A M	A M	A M	A M	A M	A M	A M	A M	A M	A M	A M	M	P M	P M	P M	P M	P M	P M	P M	P M
Lv. Dayton	0								6 00	6 22	6 45	7 07	7 30	7 52	8 15	8 37	9 00	9 22	9 45	10 07	10 30	10 52	11 15	11 37	12 00	12 22	12 45	1 07	1 30	1 52	2 15	2 37	3 00
" Calvary	2.8								6 15	6 37	7 00	7 22	7 45	8 07	8 30	8 52	9 15	9 37	10 00	10 22	10 45	11 07	11 30	11 52	12 15	12 39	1 00	1 22	1 45	2 07	2 30	2 52	3 15
" Alexandersville	7.2							5 50	6 27	6 50	7 10	7 32	7 56	8 18	8 41	9 03	9 26	9 48	10 11	10 33	10 56	11 18	11 41	12 03	12 26	12 50	1 11	1 33	1 56	2 18	2 41	3 03	3 26
" W. Carrollton	7.7							5 52	6 30	6 52	7 14	7 37	7 59	8 22	8 44	9 07	9 29	9 52	10 14	10 37	10 59	11 22	11 44	12 07	12 29	12 52	1 14	1 37	1 59	2 22	2 44	3 07	3 29
" Miamisburg	11.0						5 51	6 02	6 41	7 03	7 26	7 50	8 11	8 33	8 56	9 20	9 41	10 03	10 26	10 50	11 11	11 34	11 56	12 20	12 41	1 03	1 26	1 50	2 11	2 34	2 56	3 20	3 40
" M. & G. Jct.																																	
" Germantown	16.2											8 10				9 40				11 10				12 40				2 10				3 40	
" Chautauqua	14.3						6 01		6 51	7 13	7 36		8 21	8 43	9 05		9 51	10 13	10 36		11 21	11 44	12 06		12 51	1 13	1 35		2 21	2 43	3 06		3 51
" Franklin	17.0				5 25	5 50	6 11		6 56	7 20	7 45		8 30	8 50	9 15		10 00	10 20	10 45		11 30	11 50	12 15		1 00	1 22	1 45		2 30	2 52	3 15		4 00
" L. & F. Jct.																																	
" Red Lion	22.0					6 05				7 35				9 05				10 35				12 05				1 35				3 05			
" Lebanon	27.8					6 20				7 50				9 20				10 50				12 20				1 50				3 20			
" Middletown	23.3			5 22	5 52		6 37		7 22			8 07	8 52			9 37			11 07		11 52		12 37				1 22		2 07		2 52		4 22
" Engleside	26.6			5 30	6 02		6 47		7 32			8 17	9 02			9 47			11 17		12 02		12 47				1 32		2 17		3 02		4 32
" Trenton C. B.	27.6	4 50		5 37	6 07		6 52		7 37			8 22	9 07			9 52			11 23		12 07		12 52				1 37		2 22		3 07		4 37
" Busenbark	29.8	4 56		5 45	6 15		7 00		7 45			8 30	9 15			10 00			11 30		12 15		1 00				1 45		2 30		3 15		4 45
" Overpeck	31.9	4 58		5 47	6 17		7 02		7 47			8 32	9 17			10 02			11 32		12 17		1 02				1 47		2 32		3 17		4 47
" Ohlingers	34.0	5 03		5 53	6 23		7 08		7 53			8 38	9 23			10 08			11 38		12 23		1 08				1 53		2 38		3 23		4 53
" Hamilton	36.3	5 15		6 07	6 37		7 22		8 07			8 52	9 37			10 22			11 52		12 37		1 22				2 07		2 52		3 37		5 07
" Lindenwald	38.9	5 26	5 12	6 18	6 49		7 33		8 18			9 04	9 49			10 34			12 04		12 49		1 34				2 19		3 04		3 49		5 19
" Symmes Corner	41.0	5 30	5 16	6 22	6 52		7 37		8 22			9 07	9 52			10 37			12 07		12 52		1 37				2 22		3 07		3 52		5 22
" Pleasant Run	44.0	5 37	5 22	6 30	7 00		7 45		8 30			9 15	10 00			10 45			12 15		1 00		1 45				2 30		3 15		4 00		5 30
" New Burlington	46.9	5 45	5 28	6 37	7 07		7 52		8 37			9 22	10 07			10 52			12 22		1 07		1 52				2 37		3 22		4 07		5 37
" Mt. Healthy	48.8	5 52	5 34	6 45	7 15		8 00		8 45			9 30	10 15			11 00			12 30		1 15		2 00				2 45		3 30		4 15		5 42
" College Hill	50.9	5 57	5 39	6 49	7 19		8 04		8 49			9 34	10 19			11 04			12 34		1 19		2 04				2 49		3 34		4 19		5 46
Ar. Cincinnati	54.4	6 11		7 05	7 35		8 20		9 05			9 50	10 35			11 20			12 50		1 35		2 20				3 05		3 50		4 35		6 00
		A M	A M	A M	A M	A M	A M	A M	A M	A M	A M	A M	A M	A M	A M	A M	A M	A M	P M	A M	P M	P M	P M	P M	P M	P M	P M	P M	P M	P M	P M	P M	P M

*No. 6 Daily from Trenton. Daily except Sunday from Middletown.
*No. 8 Daily from Middletown. Daily except Sunday from Franklin.
*No. 10 Daily from Franklin. Daily except Sunday from Miamisburg.
No. 20 Daily from Franklin. Daily except Sunday from Dayton.
No. 16 will make direct connections for Germantown daily. For Lebanon Sunday only,

D—Daily. D. Ex. S.—Daily except Sunday. D. Ex. S. and S.—Daily except [Sunday and Saturday …]

C. D. & T. TRACTION CO. TR[ACTION …]

GOING NORTH BETWEEN

Cincinnati, Hamilton, Middletown, Lebanon, Franklin, Germa[ntown …]

NORTH BOUND. READ DOWN.

Station	Miles	No. 1	No. 3	No. 7	No. 11	No. 13	No. 15	No. 19	No. 23	No. 25	No. 27	No. 29	No. 31	No. 33	No. 35	No. 39	No. 41	No. 43	No. 45	No. 47	No. 49	No. 51	No. 53	No. 55	No. 57	No. 59	No. 61	No. 63	No. 65	No. 69	No. 71	No. 73
Class		D	D Ex.S	D Ex.S	D	D Fx.S	D Ex.S	D	D Ex.S	D	D	D* Ex.S	D	D	D	D	D	D	D	D	D	D	D	D	D	D	D	D	D	D	D	D
		A M	A M	A M	A M	A M	A M	A M	A M	A M	A M	A M	A M	A M	A M	A M	A M	A M	A M	A M	A M	A M	A M	A M	P M	A M	P M	A M	P M	P M	P M	P M
Lv. Cincinnati	0													6 37		7 22		8 07		8 52		9 37		10 22		11 07		11 52		12 37		1 22
" College Hill Jct.	3.5											6 10		6 52		7 37		8 22		9 07		9 52		10 37		11 22		12 07		12 52		1 37
" Mt. Healthy	5.5											6 15		7 00		7 45		8 30		9 15		10 00		10 45		11 30		12 15		1 00		1 45
" New Burlington	7.6											6 22		7 07		7 52		8 37		9 22		10 07		10 52		11 37		12 22		1 07		1 52
" Pleasant Run	10.5											6 30		7 15		8 00		8 45		9 30		10 15		11 00		11 45		12 30		1 15		2 00
" Symmes Cor.	13.2									5 50		6 35		7 20		8 05		8 50		9 35		10 20		11 05		11 50		12 35		1 20		2 05
" Lindenwald	15.6									5 56		6 40		7 25		8 10		8 55		9 40		10 25		11 10		11 55		12 40		1 25		2 10
" Hamilton	17.9									6 07		6 52		7 37		8 22		9 07		9 52		10 37		11 22		12 07		12 52		1 37		2 22
" Ohlingers	20.6									6 18		7 03		7 48		8 33		9 18		10 03		10 48		11 33		12 18		1 03		1 48		2 33
" Overpeck	22.7									6 25		7 10		7 55		8 40		9 25		10 10		10 55		11 40		12 25		1 10		1 55		2 40
" Busenbark	24.6									6 30		7 15		8 00		8 45		9 30		10 15		11 00		11 45		12 30		1 15		2 00		2 45
" Trenton	27.5		4 45	5 00	5 07			5 50		6 35		7 20		8 05		8 52		9 35		10 20		11 05		11 50		12 35		1 20		2 05		2 50
" Engleside	29.5		4 50	5 08	5 12			5 55		6 42		7 27		8 12		8 57		9 42		10 27		11 12		11 57		12 42		1 27		2 12		2 57
" Middletown	31.5		5 00	5 15	5 22			6 07		6 52		7 37		8 22		9 07		9 52		10 37		11 22		12 07		12 52		1 37		2 22		3 07
" Lebanon									6 20				7 50				9 20				10 50				12 20				1 50			
" Red Lion									6 35				8 05				9 35				11 05				12 35				2 05			
" L. & F. Junc. / Franklin	37.6		5 19	5 37	5 44			6 29	6 52	7 14		7 59	8 22	8 44		9 29	9 52	10 14		10 59	11 22	11 44		12 29	12 52	1 14		1 59	2 22	2 44		3 29
" Chautauqua	40.0		5 25	5 43	5 50			6 35	6 58	7 20		8 05	8 28	8 50		9 35	9 58	10 20		11 05	11 28	11 50		12 35	12 58	1 20		2 05	2 28	2 50		3 35
" Germantown							6 00				7 25				8 55				10 25				11 55				1 25				2 55	
" M. & G. Junc. / Miamisburg	43.6		5 40	5 50	6 02	6 17	6 25	6 48	7 10	7 33	7 50	8 18	8 40	9 03	9 20	9 48	10 10	10 33	10 50	11 18	11 40	12 03	12 20	12 48	1 10	1 33	1 50	2 18	2 40	3 03	3 20	3 48
" W. Carrollton	46.6		5 50		6 15	6 29	6 37	7 00	7 22	7 45	8 07	8 30	8 52	9 15	9 37	10 00	10 22	10 45	11 07	11 30	11 52	12 15	12 37	1 00	1 22	1 46	2 07	2 30	2 52	3 15	3 37	4 00
" Alexandersville	47.3		5 53		6 18		6 40	7 03	7 25	7 48	8 10	8 33	8 55	9 18	9 40	10 03	10 25	10 48	11 10	11 33	11 55	12 18	12 50	1 03	1 25	1 48	2 10	2 33	2 55	3 18	3 40	4 03
" Calvary	51.8	5 40	6 07		6 30		6 52	7 15	7 37	8 00	8 22	8 45	9 07	9 30	9 52	10 15	10 37	11 00	11 22	11 45	12 07	12 30	12 52	1 15	1 37	2 00	2 22	2 45	3 07	3 30	3 52	4 15
" Dayton	54.6	5 55	6 20		6 43		7 05	7 28	7 50	8 12	8 35	8 58	9 20	9 42	10 05	10 28	10 50	11 13	11 35	11 58	12 20	12 43	1 05	1 28	1 50	2 13	2 35	2 58	3 20	3 43	4 05	4 28
		A M	A M	A M	A M	A M	A M	A M	A M	A M	A M	A M	A M	A M	A M	A M	A M	A M	A M	A M	P M	P M	P M	P M	P M	P M	P M	P M	P M	P M	P M	P M

The column between No. 23 and No. 25 carries the vertical note: "Daily from Franklin / Daily Ex. Sun. from Lebanon." A further column (No. 75) runs off the right edge of the page and is not fully legible.

Passengers leave Germantown on Trains No. 101, 103, 107 and 111 transfer at Miamisburg.
Passengers leave Lebanon on Trains No. 95, 101, 107 and 113 transfer at Franklin.
Train No. 15 will leave Germantown at 6.20 a. m. Sundays, connecting at Miamisburg with Trains Nos. 16 and 19.
Train No. 105 to Hamilton Sundays only.

*Trains No. 29 daily from Symme's. Daily except Sunday from College Hill.

RAIN SERVICE

own, Hamilton and Cincinnati.

OCTOBER, 1904.

THIS TIME TABLE shows approximate time arrival and departure of trains. They are subject to change and are not guaranteed. Passengers are requested to verify the time by asking the Ticket Agent before starting.

No. 78	No. 80	No. 84	No. 86	No. 88	No. 90	No. 92	No. 94	No. 98	No. 98	No. 100	No. 100	No. 102	No. 104	No. 104	No. 106	No. 106	No. 108	No. 108	No. 110	No. 110	No. 112	No. 114	No. 114	No. 116	SOUTH BOUND. READ DOWN.
PM	PM	PM	PM	PM	PM	PM	PM	PM	PM	PM	PM	PM	PM	PM	PM	PM	PM	PM	PM	PM	PM	AM	AM	AM	
3 45	4 07	4 30	4 52	5 15	5 37		6 00	6 30		7 00		7 30	8 00		9 05		10 00		11 00			12 00			Lv. Dayton
4 00	4 22	4 45	5 07	5 30	5 52		6 15	6 44		1 15		7 45	8 12		9 17		10 12		11 12			12 12			" Calvary
4 11	4 33	4 56	5 18	5 41	6 03		6 26	6 55		7 26		7 56	8 23		9 28		10 23		11 23			12 23			" Alexandersville
4 14	4 37	4 59	5 22	5 44	6 07		6 29	7 00		7 30		7 59	8 26		9 30		10 26		11 26			12 26			" W. Carrollton
4 26	4 50	5 11	5 34	5 56	6 20		6 41	7 11		7 40	7 40	8 10	8 38		9 39	9 40	10 37	10 37	11 37	11 37		12 37	12 37		Miamitburg M. & G. Junct.
	5 10				6 40						8 02					10 00		10 58		11 58			12 58		" Germantown
4 36		5 21	5 46	6 06			6 51	7 20		7 47		8 18	8 45		9 46		10 45		11 45			12 45			" Chautauqua
4 45		5 30	5 52	6 15			7 00	7 29	7 30	7 57		8 28	8 53	9 00	9 54		10 53	11 07	11 53		12 07	13 53			Franklin L. & F. Junc.
			6 05						7 45					9 15				11 20							" Red Lion
			6 20						8 00					9 30				11 35							" Lebanon
5 07		5 52		6 37		7 07	7 22	7 52		8 22		8 50	9 15		10 15		11 15		12 15		12 32	1 04		1 47	" Middletown
5 17		6 02		6 47		7 17	7 32	8 02		8 30		9 00	9 24		10 24		11 24		12 24		12 40	1 12		1 53	" Engleside
5 22		6 07		6 52		7 22	7 37	8 07		8 35		9 05	9 30		10 30		11 30		12 30		12 45	1 15		2 00	" Trenton
5 30		6 15		7 00			7 45			8 41			9 37		10 37		11 37								" Busenbark
5 32		6 17		7 02			7 47			8 43			9 39		10 39		11 39								" Overpeck
5 38		6 23		7 08			7 53			8 49			9 45		10 45		12 45								" Ohlingers
5 52		6 37		7 22			8 05			9 00			10 00		11 00		12 00								" Hamilton
6 04		6 49		7 35			8 14			9 11			10 11		11 09		12 11								" Lindenwald
6 07		6 52		7 40			8 17			9 15			10 15		11 13		12 13								" Symmes Cor.
6 15		7 00		7 45			8 23			9 22			10 22		11 20										" Pleasant Run
6 22		7 07		7 52			8 30			9 30			10 30		11 30										" New Burlington
6 30		7 15		8 00			8 37			8 37			10 37		11 33										" Mt. Healthy
6 34		7 19		8 07			8 42			9 42			10 42		11 37										" College Hill
6 50		7 37		8 22			8 52			9 59			10 57		11 52										Ar. Cincinnati
PM	PM	PM	PM	PM	PM	PM	PM	PM	PM	PM	PM	PM	PM	PM	PM	PM	PM	PM	PM	PM	PM	AM	AM	AM	

*NOTE—Take C. D. & T. cars at Fountain Square or Clark St. cars at Cor. 6th and Walnut, and allow 45 minutes to make the connection with Main Line Cars at Spring Grove Terminal.

nd Sunday. S.—Sunday only.

N SERVICE

n, Miamisburg and Dayton.

OCTOBER, 1904.

THIS TIME TABLE shows approximate time arrival and departure of trains. They are subject to change and are not guaranteed. Passengers are requested to verify the time by asking the Ticket Agent before starting.

No. 83	No. 85	No. 87	No. 89	No. 91	No. 93	No. 93	No. 95	No. 97	No. 99	No. 101	No. 101	No. 103	No. 103	No. 105	No. 107	No. 107	No. 111	No. 111	No. 113	No. 117	No. 119	NORTH BOUND. READ DOWN.
PM	PM	PM	PM	PM	PM	PM	PM	PM	PM	PM	PM	PM	PM	PM	PM	PM	PM	PM	PM	PM	AM	
2 52		3 37		4 22	4 52		5 20	6 00	6 35	7 00		8 00		8 30	9 00		10 00			11 15	12 20	Lv. Cincinnati
3 07		3 52		4 37	5 07		5 35	6 15	6 50	7 15		8 15		8 45	9 15		10 15			11 30	12 32	" College Hill Jct.
3 15		4 00		4 45	5 15		5 42	6 30	7 00	7 25		8 22		8 52	9 22		10 22			11 33	12 40	" Mt. Healthy
3 22		4 07		4 52	5 22		5 50	6 37	7 07	7 31		8 30		9 00	9 30		10 30			11 38	12 45	" New Burlington
3 30		4 15		5 00	5 30		6 00	6 45	7 15	7 36		8 37		9 07	9 37		10 37			11 43	12 50	" Pleasant Run
3 35		4 20		5 05	5 35		6 05	6 50	7 20	7 40		8 40		9 15	9 40		10 40			11 45	12 53	" Symmes Cor.
3 40		4 25		5 10	5 41		6 10	6 55	7 25	7 45		8 47			9 47		10 47			11 50	12 58	" Lindenwald
3 52		4 37		5 22	5 52		6 22	7 07	7 37	7 55		9 00			10 00		11 00			12 00	1 10	" Hamilton
4 03		4 48		5 33	6 03		6 33	7 18	7 48	8 04		9 11			10 11		11 11			12 08	1 18	" Ohlingers
4 10		4 55		5 40	6 10		6 40	7 25	7 55	8 10		9 18			10 18		11 18			12 12	1 22	" Overpecks
4 15		5 00		5 45	6 15		6 45	7 30	8 00	8 15		9 22			10 22		11 22			12 15	1 25	" Busenbark
4 20		5 05		5 50	6 20		6 50	7 35	8 05	8 20		9 30			10 30		11 30			12 18	1 30	" Trenton
4 27		5 12		5 57	6 27		6 57	7 42	8 12	8 27		9 35			10 25		11 35			12 22	1 34	" Engleside
4 37		5 22		6 07	6 37		7 07	7 52	8 22	8 37		9 45			10 45		11 45			12 32	1 44	" Middletown
	4 50					6 25					8 10					10 15			11 35			" Lebanon
	5 05					6 40					8 25					10 30			11 47			" Red Lion
4 59	5 22	5 44		6 29	7 00	7 00		8 11		8 59	8 44	10 07			11 07	10 50	12 07		12 05			L. & F. Junc. Franklin
5 05	5 28	5 50		6 35	7 06			8 17		9 05		10 13			11 13		12 13					" Chautauqua
			5 55			6 50					8 55		10 00			11 00		12 00				" Germantown
5 18	5 40	6 03	6 20	6 48	7 18	7 12		8 27		9 18	9 15	10 22	10 20		11 22	11 20	12 22	12 20				M. & G. Junc. Miamisburg
5 30	5 52	6 15	6 37	7 00	7 30			8 35		9 30		10 34			11 34		12 34					" W. Carrollton
5 33	5 55	6 18	6 40	7 03	7 33			8 37		9 33		10 36			11 36		12 36					" Alexandersville
5 45	6 07	6 30	6 52	7 15	7 45			8 47		9 45		10 45			11 45							" Calvary
5 58	6 20	6 43	7 07	7 28	8 00			9 00		10 00		11 00			12 00							Ar. Dayton
PM	PM	PM	PM	PM	PM	PM	PM	PM	PM	PM	PM	PM	PM	PM	PM	PM	AM	AM	AM	AM	AM	

*NOTE—Take C. D. & T. cars at Fountain Square or Clark St. cars at Cor. 6th and Walnut, and allow 45 minutes to make the connection with Main Line Cars at Spring Grove Terminal.

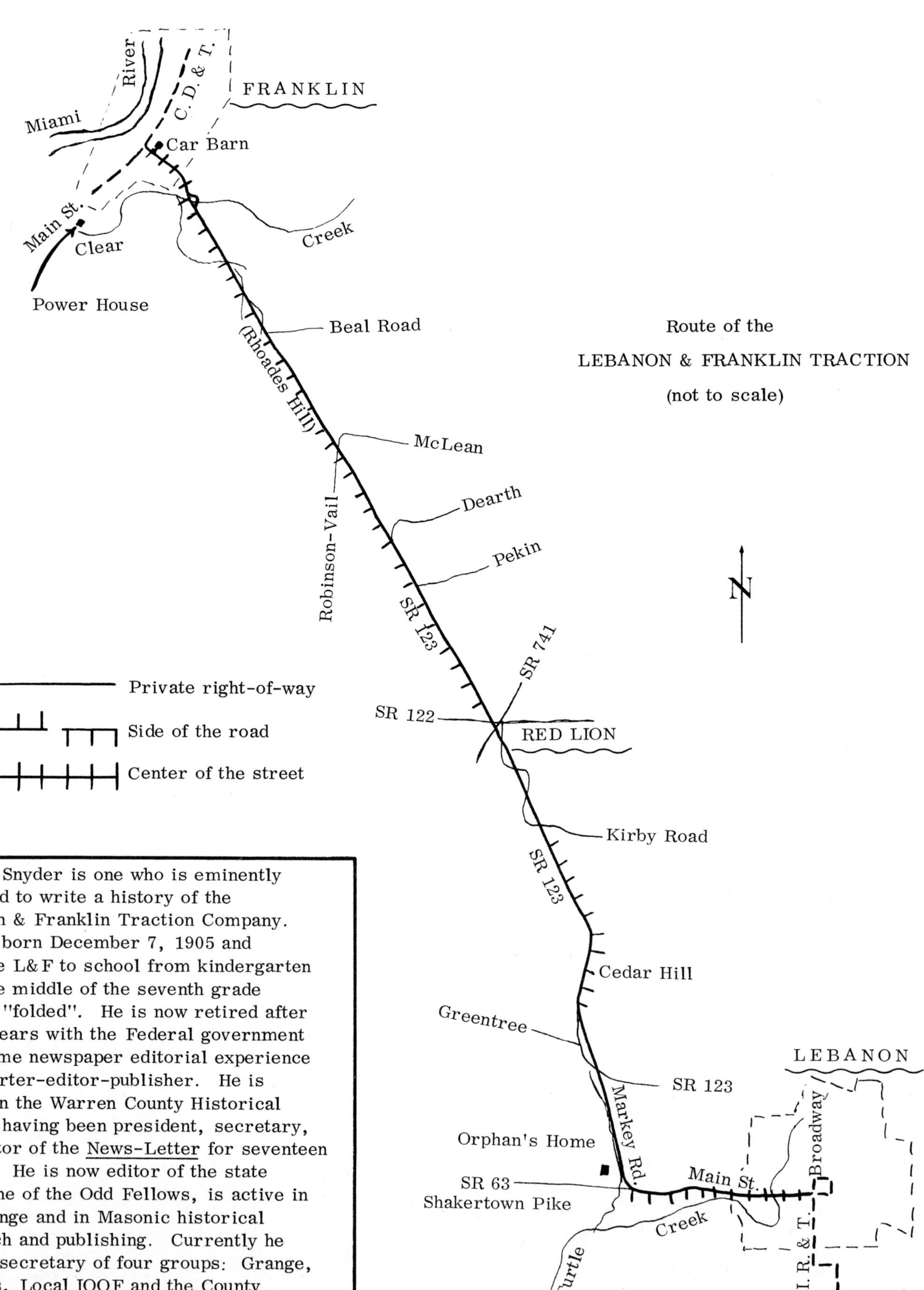

Miami
River
C. D. & T.
FRANKLIN
Car Barn
Main St.
Clear
Creek
Power House
Beal Road
(Rhoades Hill)
Route of the
LEBANON & FRANKLIN TRACTION
(not to scale)
McLean
Dearth
Robinson-Vail
Pekin
SR 123
SR 741
SR 122
RED LION
N
Private right-of-way
Side of the road
Center of the street
Kirby Road
SR 123
Cedar Hill
Greentree
SR 123
LEBANON
Orphan's Home
Markey Rd.
Broadway
SR 63
Shakertown Pike
Main St.
Creek
Turtle
I. R. & T.

Marion Snyder is one who is eminently
qualified to write a history of the
Lebanon & Franklin Traction Company.
He was born December 7, 1905 and
rode the L&F to school from kindergarten
until the middle of the seventh grade
when it "folded". He is now retired after
thirty years with the Federal government
plus some newspaper editorial experience
as reporter-editor-publisher. He is
active in the Warren County Historical
Society having been president, secretary,
and editor of the News-Letter for seventeen
years.   He is now editor of the state
magazine of the Odd Fellows, is active in
the Grange and in Masonic historical
research and publishing. Currently he
is also secretary of four groups: Grange,
Kiwanis, Local IOOF and the County
board of mental retardation. He and
Mrs. Snyder have two sons and he must
take time from his activities to enjoy their
four grandchildren sometimes!

THE LEBANON & FRANKLIN TRACTION COMPANY

By MARION SNYDER, Lebanon, Ohio

Beset by a variety of problems from the day of its conception through its birth, fourteen-plus years of active life, and then sudden death and oblivion, the Lebanon & Franklin Traction line has been passed over by Ohio historians, even traction line writers.

Its birth came in an era beset by the robust expansion of the electric railway which brought the rattle and bang of trolley wheels throughout the nation, particularly in the midwest, and southwestern Ohio was no exception. A group of Dayton investors had erected a short line from Miamisburg to Germantown and later sold it to the Southern Ohio Traction Company which ran from Cincinnati north through Hamilton, Middletown, Franklin, and Miamisburg to Dayton, then on to Columbus and Toledo.

Robert E. Kline headed the Gem City combine that was now looking for a fresh opportunity to construct a similar line. They felt that a ten-mile run from Franklin to Lebanon was the answer. Already other groups had visions of other lines into Lebanon. Of the four lines projected for the "seat of worth" in Warren County, two came into reality. These were the Rapid Railway division of Interurban Railway & Terminal from Cincinnati, the other the Lebanon-Franklin line.

This all-Warren County line would give Lebanonites as well as those residing near the projected line an opportunity for quick (by 1900 standards) egress to Dayton, Middletown or Hamilton. Visions of heavy freight traffic as well as passenger patronage were like "stars in the eyes" of the Dayton investors.

The first mention in a Lebanon newspaper uncovered by the author is in the issue of November 28, 1901 when a small article ends with the observation that "the proposed line from Franklin to Lebanon should be built." The issue dated January 8, 1903, fourteen months later, stated there was "still hope for the Lebanon and Franklin trolley."

By this time the promoters, having failed to obtain a green light from the county commissioners to lay their rails along side the main road between the two communities, were busy buying rights of way. Meanwhile an effort was being made to push for a line to be built direct from Dayton through Centerville to Lebanon but it never materialized.

Rights of way for the most part came easy as farmers along the way wanted the new enterprise to pass their doors, which in some instances was literally true when a farm residence was near the highway now known as Ohio 123. However, the line coming southeast after skirting Red Lion (about half

The hill on State Route 123 is easily traveled in 1974 by motorists who may be unaware of how the L&F traction cars labored to climb it at times when power was low. The traction line was on the left side of the road (looking north). (R. M. Wagner)

way between the two towns) was laid out to go in a direct line to the junction of Kirby Road with the present Ohio 123. This called for it to cut through one tillable field on the Ben Blackburn farm and to cut two fields on the George Tilton farm into four, thus bringing on a law suit which, however, did not stop the line's construction.

The actual grading for the new line started midway between Franklin and Red Lion near the crest of Rhoades hill. This elevation was to be the biggest engineering problem in building the road, and later cars found it difficult to surmount when power was low or there was ice on the rails. Power difficulties were not to be uncommon. Power was purchased from the Southern Ohio line, by then known as the Cincinnati, Dayton & Toledo, which had problems at times providing power to the "branch line".

The second hill, not to be as steep a grade but one that proved a problem to make on many occasions, was known to the traction employees as "Cedar Hill". This was in front of the farm of the author's grandfather who had planted a row of cedars just inside his fence along the road from the foot of the hill to a couple hundred feet past its top.

A car Lebanon-bound "had it made" if it could make it up Rhoades hill; on the return trip it was "home free" after passing Cedar Hill. In the six-plus years that the author rode this traction to school in Lebanon, the cars often experienced difficulty at the latter hill as my stop was near its base. As I grew older the car would not stop but when it slowed down at the steep part of the hill I would swing off, always safely.

I also recall that when power was low, the car would creep especially slow and the high school boys would like to tease the motorman by getting off, walking to the top, and then climbing back on.

The route followed by the line started at its Franklin office at Sixth and Main streets (which was also the "main line's" office) coming east over Sixth, over Clear Creek, and on the west side of the highway to Red Lion, then cut due southeast (twice crossing present Ohio 123) to the junction of the west end of Kirby Road and the highway; then it ran along the east side of the highway south until it swerved to the left and cut through the pasture field of the Mulford farm and again crossed the highway where Markey Road presently junctions with Ohio 123. Then it ran directly south and east of the road then called "Orphans Home" road, now Markey road, until it came to Shakertown Pike, now Ohio 63. It crossed that pike, turned left and ran along the south side until it reached Lebanon, then down Main Street to its terminus at Broadway. The Rapid Railway line, which started operations in late September 1903, ran over Broadway so that passengers had but half a block to go to board a trolley for Cincinnati.

The work of grading got under way in earnest in early July, 1903, although some dirt was moved near the William Ivins farm in June. Grading was

A "cut" for the roadbed can still be seen at the top of Rhoades Hill in 1974.

At the bottom of the hill was a "fill" to raise the roadbed and ease the grade. The railway's stone abutment remains.

Across from the abutment, the traction roadbed has already (after 55 years) been cut into for a land development. (All three, R. M. Wagner)

The Lebanon & Franklin traction line began in Franklin on Sixth Street along side of the station which it shared with the electric line traveling on Main Street in front of the station. That line was part of the Ohio Electric Railway at the time of this picture. The L&F car barn was on Sixth Street near the station and can be seen on the right with a phone booth at its side. (Richard A. Lenehan)

accomplished by moving dirt with horse drawn scoops. These were generally from farmers nearby glad for a chance to make some extra money. The exact wage paid is not certain but the Rapid Railway paid four dollars per day for a man and a team. However, an extra man was needed to bear down the scoop handles in loading it. Sometimes in tough places, a second team would be hitched on; this team was the "snatch team" and could be either two or three horses. After loading it was unhitched and the process repeated with another scoop. Wheel scoops were the best for this type work; just about every farmer had a scoop of some sort. The snatch team and its driver drew five dollars per day, a six day week bringing in thirty dollars, rather good wages for those days back in 1903. The days were usually ten hours long.

However, the grading was not very far along when the promoters ran into financial trouble and work was stopped for a brief time while an $87,000 bond issue was floated to keep the line in business. This was accomplished through the Citizens National Bank in Lebanon, now consolidated with the present Lebanon-Citizens National Bank. The consolidation had no relation to the rail firm's financial difficulties.

Early predictions of the date when operations would begin were before Christmas in 1903. It was not to occur until five months later. Prospective patrons had to use some patience as work progressed rather slowly. The Red Lion correspondent of the Western Star (weekly newspaper) at Lebanon reported in the issue of December 24, 1903 that "Our citizens are awaiting the happening of two events--Santa Claus and the arrival of the first car from Franklin."

A month later the same correspondent reported that, "We are still waiting anxiously for the first car to pass over the traction line to arrive in our midst..." Winter weather held back work considerably but the line received a terrific blow on March 25, 1904 when a heavy rainstorm and the resulting high water took out the line's $5,000 bridge over Clear Creek at Franklin.

However, the damage was caused by an uprooted tree some twelve feet across at its roots and five

Like the railway, whose advent was celebrated within its walls, the old spired opera house is gone.
It stood on the northeast corner of Broadway and Main in Lebanon on the opposite side of the street
from the famed hotel, the Golden Lamb, which was then called the Lebanon House.   The traction
approached this intersection from the west and its tracks ended in Main Street along side of the hotel.
(Both, Warren County Historical Society)

and a half feet in diameter. Despite the rather slow progress one newspaper account dated April 7, 1904 felt that "considering the long, cold weather (winter) when work on the road lay idle, the company made great progress." Finally all the loose ends were put together and the promoters began making plans for celebrating the work's completion and the advent of the first car into Lebanon.

This happened on Saturday, May 28, and the car, including my father (he wasn't married yet), arrived in the county seat. Thus Lebanon welcomed its second traction line in nine months, as the Rapid Railway began services the end of the previous September.

Personnel of the various committees formed for the gala event scheduled at the Opera House (Lebanon's "Town Hall"), read like a "Who's Who" in Lebanon. The date was set for June 3.

The firm purchased two new cars for its operations. They were numbered 103 and 104, one having a baggage compartment. The cars made in Dayton were reported by the Western Star to be "Splinter new, having left the Dayton shops Friday evening.

The trip (from Franklin) is now 45 minutes but this will soon be reduced to thirty minutes and through cars to Dayton put on."

The gala banquet and program on June 3 was catered by the Ludlum Brothers of Lebanon and music was furnished by the town's leading bandsman, Ben Lewis. The cars brought some 75 persons here from Franklin and 50 from Dayton, plus a few from Cincinnati besides local dignitaries. A lengthy program followed the banquet, the affair breaking up at 11:25 p.m. to allow the traction riders to make the 11:30 (last car) departure time.

The banquet program included numerous toasts and speeches of varying lengths. These included "Let Us Get in Touch" by John Harding; "The Lebanon & Franklin Traction" by Chester H. Bosler, the line's Dayton attorney and an investor; "A Passing Type" by Lebanon's Seth W. Brown, one time congressman; "The Vicissitudes of Trolley Building" by Robert E. Kline, president of the firm.

Also heard were "Power House" by Ralph B. Parks; "The Tie That Binds" by Franklin Chronicle editor S. S. Tibbals; "Medical Profession, A Potent

Factor in Securing Unity" by Dr. Otho Evans; this trio being from Franklin. Lebanon physician Dr. C. A. Hough spoke on "Magnetism". The good doctor even then was trying to get a line into Lebanon from either Dayton or Xenia.

Prior to the banquet the visitors, arriving on the two new cars, were taken on an hour's ride about Lebanon. Reports are that covers were laid for 240 persons. The orchestra was on the front of the large stage and the decorations were profusely arranged in the form of bunting and American flags. White and pink roses provided the table decorations.

The cars were manned by teams of a motorman and a conductor. Usually a conductor could operate the car if need be as it was no complicated operation. The line had no turn arounds; the motorman would change ends by lifting his removable controller and putting it in place at the opposite end of the car and, after changing trolley poles, proceed from there.

Their tour of duty was from noon to noon and then off the same length of time. The last car usually was in the Franklin car barn by 12:30 a. m. and the crew had to be back shortly before six to start the new day. There was quite a turnover in personnel; the two best known men were motorman Fred Blus (worthy of a magazine article himself) and Charlie Kohr, everyone's favorite conductor. Kohr had the privilege of helping build the line, serving as a conductor all its lifetime, and helping to dismantle it. Others associated with the line were Bill Wittlinger, Perry Swartzel, Leslie Blore, and William Swink to name a few.

Many traveling salesmen ("drummers" those days) rode the line as did many National Normal University students. The normal school became a World War I victim and merged with Wilmington College a year and a half before the line ceased operating.

Being only a branch line, so to speak, the Lebanon & Franklin line carried few notables. However there were a few of varying degrees of status, including a president-to-be, Warren G. Harding, if

On Broadway in Lebanon tracks of the Rapid Railway passed the hotel and curved eastward onto Main Street. There was no physical connection with tracks of the L&F which ended on west Main Street before they came to Broadway. Actually Lebanon's two interurbans were of different track gauges, the L&F being 4'-8½" and the Rapid Railway 5'-2½" wide. (Warren County Historical Society)

In Franklin at Sixth and Main F&L's double-end combine No. 104 was ready for the return trip to Lebanon after its crew had their pictures taken.   Conductor Charles Kohr is on the right. The wood pilot was mounted on the car about 1910.   (R. M. Wagner Collection)

The Lebanon & Franklin Traction Co.
Time Table

In Effect Sunday, April 4, 1909.

SOUTHBOUND			NORTHBOUND		
CARS LEAVE		ARRIVE	LEAVE	ARRIVE	ARRIVE
DAYTON	FRANKLIN	LEBANON	LEBANON	FRANKLIN	DAYTON
	5 50 am	6 20 am	6 25 am	6 55 am	7 58 am
6 00 am	7 05 am	7 35 am	7 55 am	8 25 am	9 28 am
7 30 am	8 35 am	9 05 am	9 25 am	9 55 am	10 58 am
9 00 am	10 05 am	10 35 am	10 55 am	11 25 am	12 28 pm
10 30 am	11 35 am	12 05 pm	12 25 pm	12 55 pm	1 58 pm
12 00 noon	1 05 pm	1 35 pm	1 55 pm	2 25 pm	3 28 pm
1 30 pm	2 35 pm	3 05 pm	3 25 pm	3 55 pm	4 58 pm
3 00 pm	4 05 pm	4 35 pm	4 55 pm	5 25 pm	6 28 pm
4 30 pm	5 35 pm	6 05 pm	6 25 pm	6 55 pm	7 58 pm
6 00 pm	7 05 pm	7 35 pm	7 55 pm	8 25 pm	9 58 pm
8 00 pm	9 05 pm	9 35 pm	10 15 pm	10 45 pm	11 58 pm
10 00 pm	11 05 pm	11 35 pm	11 35 pm	12 05 pm	

Trains Connect with Trains on the Ohio Electric Ry. Co. at Franklin.
TIME TABLE SUBJECT TO CHANGE WITHOUT NOTICE.

FRANKLIN TICKET OFFICE and WAITING ROOM
BRUBAKERS' RESTAURANT
CORNER SIXTH AND MAIN STS.

Cars leaving Middletown after the theatre make direct connection with last car for Lebanon.

LEBANON TICKET OFFICE and WAITING ROOM
LEBANON HOUSE,

Cars make connection at Franklin with north and south bound cars of the Ohio Electric Ry. Co. at Sixth Street, Franklin, Ohio.

The F&L connection with the "main line" (the Ohio Electric Railway here in early September, 1910) was a sweeping curve from Sixth Street onto Main Street in Franklin. Double-end coach 103 has just left the main line to head for Lebanon. The trolley wheel can be seen on the overhead wire. (R. M. Wagner Collection)

an interview with a one-time employee of the line is to be believed.

William "Bill" Wittlinger worked on both this line and the main line (Cincinnati & Lake Erie), being principally a maintenance man with the branch line. However when the occasion demanded Wittlinger would fill in as a motorman, having operated a work car many times.

In an interview with a <u>Middletown Journal</u> reporter some twenty years after the line had ceased operations Wittlinger claimed that he was called upon to make a charter run from the Franklin car barn to Lebanon to pick up Marion, Ohio's first citizen of that day, Warren Gamaliel Harding, yet to make his mark on national politics but well known in Ohio by that time.

According to Wittlinger, Harding was in southwest Ohio to campaign for his nephew, G. E. "Gene" Harding, then running for congress from the third district. After completing his campaigning, in the company of R. C. Dowling, identified by Wittlinger only as assistant postmaster (stationed at Middletown), Harding rode the Rapid Railway trolley to Kings Mills to visit Colonel George G. King, son of the founder of the powder company for which the town was named. The visit was no doubt of a politcal nature as Colonel King was one of the Republican chieftains in Warren County. Although this county was not in his nephew's district, Warren G. may well have been looking to the future. This was the campaign of 1906, the state elections having been changed after 1905 to coincide with the national elections; so it was 1908 before a new state ticket would be placed before the voters.

Harding had served as lieutenant governor and it was several years before he would find himself

Only $2\frac{1}{2}$ miles north of Franklin was the Chautauqua station from which traction passengers could cross a foot bridge into the Miami Valley Chautauqua grounds. On the left are tracks of the New York Central Railroad. (R. M. Wagner Coll.)

elected U. S. Senator and eight years later "railroaded", so to speak, into the White House. But he was in politics plenty in the interim, being a fine orator and a knowledgeable politician. After the pair visited Colonel King, they came to Lebanon on the Rapid Railway and transferred to the waiting L&F charter. Wittlinger, like other traction employees, was not above slowing the car to a mere crawl, opening the front window and somehow coming up with a shotgun to knock off a rabbit dazed by the headlights.

Wittlinger claims he asked his noted passengers if they minded him shooting a rabbit or two for his table and that Harding quickly assented and enjoyed the experience. Wittlinger also claimed that Harding remembered the incident all his life. However early research has found no mention of the incident in the Lebanon newspapers.

Charlie Kohr told the writer that Wendell Wilkie, a 1940 presidential hopeful, rode the line once to come to Lebanon to see if he would be interested in enrolling at the National Normal University but no printed record is at hand. Kohr recalled that when William Jennings Bryan came to speak at Chautauqua, near Franklin, one of the L&F cars, then not in use, was used to run the silver-tongued orator the few miles to the Chautauqua bridge where the Ohio Electric had a stop. (That bridge was doomed to be swept away in the 1913 flood.) Kohr did not recall the exact date.

On a few occasions snow stopped service on the line; one time was on February 12, 1912. The Franklin-bound car became stuck in the snow near the George Tilton residence and the crewmen stayed in the Tilton barn for two days. The passengers, two Franklin attorneys and several university students, walked to Franklin or were able to return to Lebanon.

The line occasionally transported human corpses and Mr. Kohr reported that fourteen were hauled in all, approximately one per year. One was aboard at the time the car was stalled in the snow near the Tilton residence.

Freight hauled was chiefly farm produce but some mercantile items were carried, particularly from Franklin to Red Lion for the latter's community grocery store. Farm produce placed on the Lebanon-bound car was usually destined for Cincinnati and consisted chiefly of milk, cream, eggs, chickens in coops, and an occasional bawling calf. Franklin-bound cars leaned more to farm produce intended for a Dayton destination.

When the Thomson family in Middletown had a child in delicate health, his parents ordered special fresh certified milk from the French-Bauer dairy to be put on the traction car at Lebanon and then to be transferred to an Ohio Electric car for delivery in Middletown. Their son grew to be a responsible citizen and still remembers gratefully this service of the interurban in his childhood.

Dr. James H. Arnold of Lebanon was a member of a high school baseball team before World War I. He recalled that when the team had a game scheduled at Hamilton the traction provided transportation.

The bridge over the Great Miami River was washed away in the 1913 flood. The car here is an Ohio Electric type later used in Dayton suburban service. The Miami & Erie Canal in the foreground is at a higher level than the road beyond. Five modes of transportation almost touched-- river, traction, highway, canal, and steam railroad. (R. M. Wagner Collection)

One car became a popular eating place known as Mrs. Lucas's diner. At the time of these pictures (March 3, 1952) it was used for storage behind the home of Miss Newman at 620 River Street, not far from where it used to run. (R. M. Wagner)

The car was late coming to Lebanon from Franklin and the players were getting edgy because they had to make a connection with the Dayton to Cincinnati car in Franklin that would land them in Hamilton in time for a daytime game (whoever thought of night baseball in 1916-17?).

The two-man crew usually had a layover but on being late on this occasion started back to Franklin when the passengers were all on board. When the motorman was informed of the necessity of making the connection at Franklin he proved to be "a good sport"; however, Dr. Arnold said he nearly overdid it. The obliging engineer (if you want to call him that) sent the car at breakneck speed and the doctor never understood how the car was kept from jumping the track. Dr. Arnold didn't recall anything about the game (he didn't say who won) but he did vividly remember that "wild ride to Franklin".

Wilbur Swink, a teenager at the time, recalled that the snow was falling in large quantities on a certain December day in 1917 when the temperature dipped way below zero and nearly all activity was cancelled until residents could "dig out from under" a snowfall that was fence post high.

His father, William Swink, a long time employee of the traction line, was on a run from Lebanon with motorman Charlie Kohr, when one of the car's motors burned out and the car could not pull Cedar Hill, the only steep grade on the Lebanon-Franklin run. The crew returned to Lebanon and telephoned Franklin for assistance.

Fritz Blus was available in Franklin but it was a company rule that no car be taken out, even on an emergency run, without a two-man crew and no one else was available. Blus persuaded young Swink, who had worked on the road in the summer months, to be the required number two crewman.

However, the rescue car was unable to pull the crippled car up Cedar Hill and the men eventually gave up and started back to Franklin. However, the snow had fallen so heavily and drifted to such an extent that when Blus' rescue car returned north it became snowbound near the George Tilton farm six miles from Franklin. The passengers they had rescued walked the rest of the way to Franklin but Blus, Swink and Kohr stayed with the car all night and were given breakfast by the Tilton Family. At daylight they, too, made the snowy hike to Franklin.

Even an abandoned and abused car body can yield much data to a dedicated railfan--dimensions, window spacing, and even color for a good detective. All findings confirmed that the cars were forest green. (R. M. Wagner)

Combine 104 was built for the Lebanon & Franklin Traction Company in 1904 by the Barney & Smith
Car Company in Dayton. Its sister car, No. 103, was a coach and had no baggage compartment.
Note the gold double stripes and intricate designs in the corners; also note the small light in the
center end window at the top. This was probably a marker light which could be changed to a tail
light by flipping a colored disc to make it red. The fender was later replaced by a wood pilot.
(Tom Scholey, R. M. Wagner Collection)

Wilbur Swink recalled that his father stayed with the disabled car at the foot of Cedar Hill for five days then "limped" back to Lebanon with it. He then took the traction (IR&T) to Cincinnati and returned to Franklin over the Ohio Electric "main line".

There was a station in Red Lion in later years, a one-room building without heat whose doors and windows were open to the elements, which Ruth Ivins Dakin had reason to remember. She and Esther Monfort, both teachers, had to catch the first car leaving Lebanon on school days and upon reaching the Red Lion station would sit on milk cans (awaiting transportation to market or empties awaiting return to nearby farms) until it was daylight and they could see to safely walk to their respective schools. Waiting for the traction to return them to Lebanon in the evening, in cool weather they sought refuge in a brick farm house a short distance away.

The line was never without financial woes and in the days just prior to our nation getting into World War I, it was becoming apparent the traction line was "doomed" everywhere. The villain was the combustion engine--the automobile and truck were soon to push traction lines aside in their mad rush to universal popularity.

The line raised its fares and put what economy measures into effect it could but the automobile was here to stay. When the owners petitioned the Public Utilities Commission to abandon the F&L, Lebanon, Franklin, Middletown and other business men went to Columbus to protest, but their efforts were in vain.

The last day of operation was December 31, 1918. I did not ride the last car out. At 13 I was still a homebody and satisfied myself with riding it home at 3:55 p.m., the time I usually rode it on my way home from school.

When the line was being dismantled, the farmers along the route were given a chance to buy crossties, power poles and the like. The ties were ten cents each and the poles a quarter. Many ties were too far decayed to be sold but somehow disappeared from the landscape. The steel rails were sold for scrap, reportedly by their purchaser to Japanese interests.

The tearing up of the line took about two months and the real estate involved reverted to its former owners. The Tilton family was the most pleased as they were able to return their two fields to more practical operation.

The two new "splinter new" cars were used throughout the life of the line and when it ceased operation they were sold to two Franklin men for $50 each, retired from trolley runs and converted into domestic uses.

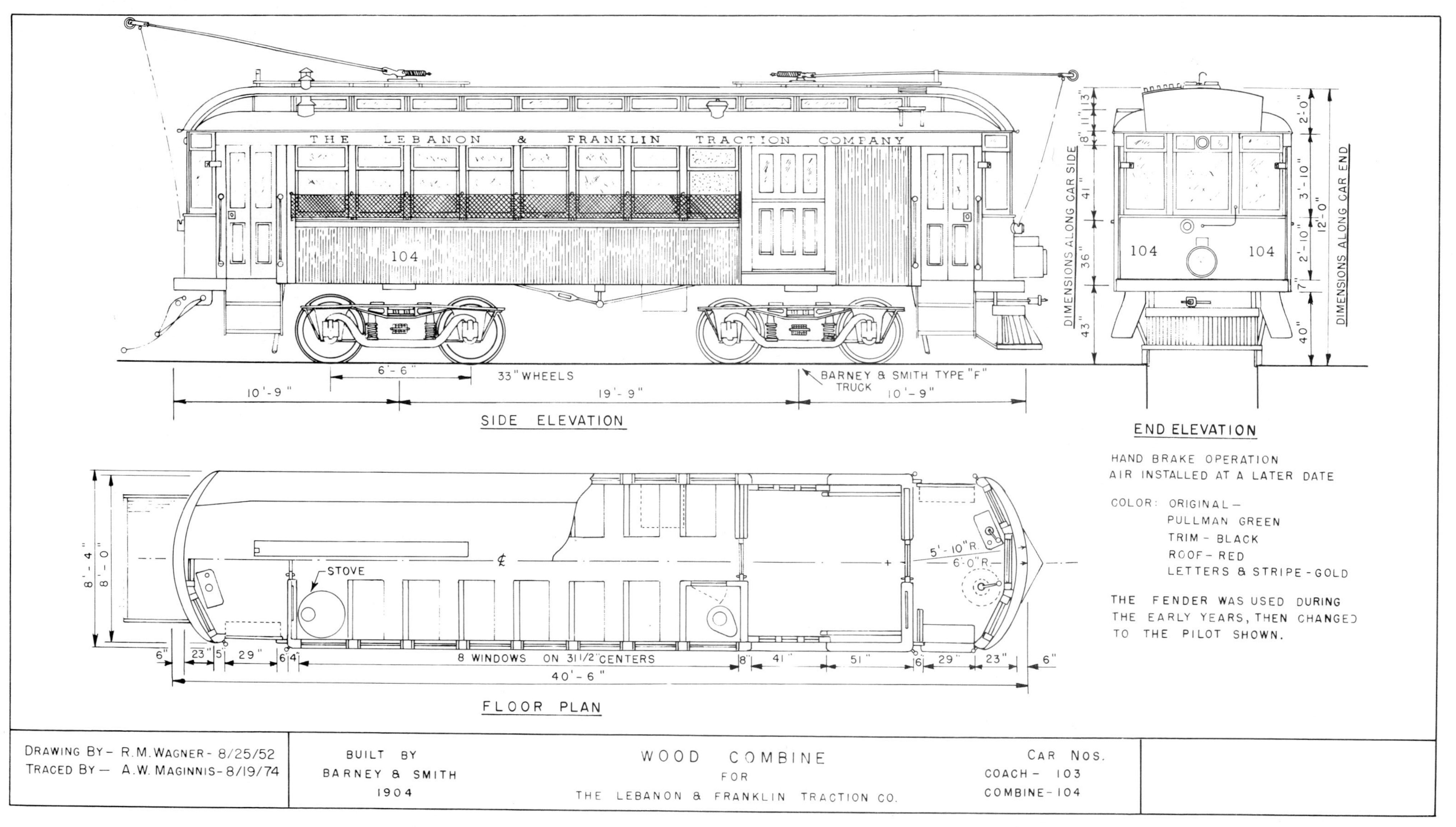
THE LEBANON & FRANKLIN TRACTION COMPANY
104
DIMENSIONS ALONG CAR SIDE
8" 11 13"
41"
36"
43"
2'-0"
3'-10"
2'-10"
7"
12'-0"
40"
DIMENSIONS ALONG CAR END
104   104
6'-6"
33" WHEELS
19'-9"
10'-9"
BARNEY & SMITH TYPE "F" TRUCK
10'-9"
SIDE ELEVATION
END ELEVATION
HAND BRAKE OPERATION
AIR INSTALLED AT A LATER DATE
COLOR: ORIGINAL —
PULLMAN GREEN
TRIM — BLACK
ROOF — RED
LETTERS & STRIPE — GOLD
THE FENDER WAS USED DURING
THE EARLY YEARS, THEN CHANGED
TO THE PILOT SHOWN.
8'-4"
8'-0"
STOVE
5'-10"R.
6'-0"R.
6" 23" 5" 29" 6 4"
8 WINDOWS ON 31/2" CENTERS
40'-6"
8' 41" 51" 6" 29" 23" 6"
FLOOR PLAN
DRAWING BY — R.M. WAGNER — 8/25/52
TRACED BY — A.W. MAGINNIS — 8/19/74
BUILT BY
BARNEY & SMITH
1904
WOOD COMBINE
FOR
THE LEBANON & FRANKLIN TRACTION CO.
CAR NOS.
COACH — 103
COMBINE — 104

TRACING THE TRACTION

in 1 9 7 4

From the above historic landmark
in Lebanon, the Golden Lamb Hotel
on Broadway, State Route 63 points
west.   That is Main Street where
the Lebanon & Franklin traction
line ended.   Going out Route 63 to
where the railway turned north on
Markey Road, the Boy Scouts
erected a marker to the memory
of the electric railway.
(Both, R. M. Wagner)

Before the bend on Markey Road an abutment can be seen. When there are no leaves on the trees the right-of-way is clearly visible.

The railway stayed on the east side of the creek. Following Markey Road and looking closely, a concrete abutment such as this is found to have survived for 55 years after the last traction car passed over it. (All three, R. M. Wagner)

At Red Lion the tracks cut across the fields and did not follow the sharp turns of the road.

Evidence of the graded right-of-way still appears on the slopes between Red Lion and Franklin and traction fans will find it easy to follow the line almost all the way to Clear Creek. Beyond that the eastern edge of Franklin has changed and traces are lost. The car barn on Sixth Street was torn down this year-- before it could be photographed. (R. M. Wagner)

On Main Street in Franklin, a few blocks south of Sixth Street where the Lebanon & Franklin tracks joined the main line, the former power house still stands. Additions have been made but the original building is easly identifiable and it still has the three apertures where the power lines passed through its brick walls. (R. M. Wagner)

CARS OF THE "MAIN LINE"

This deck roof car was a sister to car 14 of the Miamisburg & Germantown Traction Company, and was built by the Kuhlman Car Company in 1898. This type of car was used in suburban service to transport workers to the National Cash Register Company on South Main Street in Dayton.
(Thomas Scholey)

"Fast Line" cars shown here were built by the Barney & Smith Company for the Cincinnati & Miami Valley Traction Company which was organized in 1896 with M. J. Mandelbaum as president and F. T. Pomeroy as secretary and treasurer. In 1900 this company consolidated with the Dayton Traction Company, organized 1893, and the Cincinnati & Hamilton Electric Street Railway, organized 1897, to form the Southern Ohio Traction Company, predecessor of the Cincinnati, Dayton & Toledo Traction and subsequently the Ohio Electric Railway.
(Both, Barney Neuburger)

A glimpse of the Barney & Smith cars in service shows car 33, left, and car 26 at the shops in Trenton north of Hamilton. Cars of the Lebanon & Franklin would have been sent to this location for repairs.
(Both, Electric Railway Journal, 1898)

One of the deck roof Kuhlman cars stopped at Lindenwald near Williams Street. The conductor was No. 1088, Mr. Babcock, but the Ohio Electric motorman remains un-identified. (Neil Weber Collection)

South of Dayton the Ohio Electric Railway shops were located at O'Neil's--on the southwest corner of Dixie Highway and Dorothy Lane. The big car in the center, painted orange and cream, would have run on the main line, known as the Cincinnati & Dayton Traction Company after the breaking apart of the huge Ohio Electric Railway in 1918. The Cincinnati & Dayton lasted until 1926 when it became the Cincinnati, Hamilton & Dayton Railway Company under new ownership, which then proceded to reorganize into the Cincinnati & Lake Erie Railroad in 1929. (R. M. Wagner)

On the main line in the
city of Dayton Ohio
Electric car 48 waits
on Main Street at Third
Street in 1914. (Ed
Williams Collection)

On South Main Street
OE car 20 follows a
city car, a four-wheel
Dayton Street Railway
car, waiting for a freight
train crossing at grade.
(Reed C. Prugh, L. P.
Cummings Collections)

Acknowledgments: In addition to the excellent texts, pictures and data furnished by the two authors, Herb Pence, Jr. and Marion Snyder, others have helped with photographs, historical data, verifications and hours of research much of which has drawn a blank for the era of our two Ohio tractions. We extend thanks to C. L. Bandy, L. P. Cummings, Franklin Public Library, Richard A. Lenehan, Russell Lyle, David L. McNeil, Eldon Neff, Reed C. Prugh, Warren County Historical Society, Neil Weber, and Ed Williams. Car plans were drawn by A. W. Maginnis. Maps, typesetting, and layout by Birdella Wagner.

Any information about the cars and operations of the "Main Line" or pictures of the cars and scenes of the right-of-way in the era before 1920 that could be loaned to the editor would be greatly appreciated. Send to: Richard M. Wagner, 59 Euclid Avenue, Cincinnati, Ohio 45215.

Other Titles of TRACTION INTEREST by the same publisher:

THE OVERLOOK ROUTE, THE DAYTON, COVINGTON & PIQUA TRACTION CO. by William Reed Gordon and Richard M. Wagner. Overlooking the Stillwater River Valley was a 34-mile line in west central Ohio that outlasted the steam railroad that paralled it. Reminisce with traction fans of the twenties. Map, 75 pictures, 52 pages, $3.75.

CINCINNATI STREETCARS is a series by Roy J. Wright and Richard M. Wagner.

No. 1 HORSECARS AND STEAM DUMMIES
    1888 centennial map included. 28 pages, $2.00.

No. 2 THE INCLINES, transporting citizens from the basin to the hilltops which had glamorous resorts. 48 pages. $3.35.

No. 3 CABLE CARS AND EARLIEST ELECTRICS Open summer cars and closed cars. 64 pages. $3.75.

No. 4 MILLCREEK VALLEY LINES. Their cars ran from the Cincinnati Zoo to the suburbs and as far as Hamilton. A legal dispute over trolley wires. 40 pages. $3.25.

No. 5 1895 - 1911. Corporate history, high-water cars, interurbans that entered the city, Fountain Square scenes, Chester Park, etc. 72 pages. $4.25.

No. 6 1912 - 1922. Strikes, flood, war, track diagrams, historic scenes. 80 pages. $4.50.

CURVED-SIDE CARS BUILT BY CINCINNATI CAR COMPANY by Richard and Birdella Wagner, a distinctive design that became known as "rubber stamp" which ran in various cities in the States and Canada. 120 pages, vinyl cover. $9.00.

TROLLEY TALK. Reprints of a periodical with historical backgrounds, dimensions and pictures of electric railway equipment to guide model builders.

VOLUME I, No.s 1-20, 1954-1958. Basic and fundamental features of trolley cars. Imported models. 100 pages. $4.75.

VOLUME II, Nos. 21-40, 1959-1962. Trackwork, overhead, trestles, bridges, car barns. 136 pages. $6.00.

VOLUME III, Nos. 41-60, 1962-1966. Models and their prototypes. Dr. Prugh's Dayton & Western model in color. Snow sweepers, interurban piggybacks, work equipment. 156 pages. $7.50.

VOLUME IV, Nos. 61-80, 1966-1970. Histories of Dayton, Detroit, Portland, Atlantic City and Philadelphia. City cars, interurbans, streamliners and work cars. 194 pages. $9.00.

McGRAW ELECTRIC RAILWAY DIRECTORY, 1924. A high quality reprint of a priceless reference. Data includes destinations, mileage, the location of power houses and repair shops, track gauges, how much rolling stock, parent and subsidiary companies in United States, Canada, Mexico and West Indies. Hard cover $9.50, paper $6.00.

CARS AND CAR EQUIPMENT, Westinghouse special publication of October 1924 reproduced in two colors. Cars of ten states have pictures and data. 20 pages, 16 pictures, 15 plueprints. $2.00.

TROLLEY TALK

59 Euclid Avenue
Wyoming, Ohio 45215